MALCONTENT

POEMS BY

Jeffrey Charles Naish

NFB
<<<>>>
Buffalo, NY

Printed in the United States of America

Naish, Jeffrey Charles

Malcontent/ Naish- 1st Edition

ISBN: 978-0692252147

1. Malcontent – Poetry– Verse.
No Frills.
Title

Cover Image by Clarence Rhym

No Frills Buffalo
119 Dorchester Buffalo, New York 14213
For more information visit
Nofrillsbuffalo.com

"Hold onto and value
The love you find in this world,
For many will never know how it feels"

- *Scott Vogel*

1

OLD SOUL CONTINUUM, NEW WORLD PERDITION

The Age of Dumb

It doesn't take a doctorate
To see that mentally
Mankind is in the midst
Of a downward spiral.

If not for bone and gristle
Half of the world's problems
Would simply sink
Into a storm drain.

Witless lumps of flesh, enslaved
In the name of progress
Feeding the faculties
A primitive program.

No sex without debauchery.
No democracy without dishonesty.
No loyalty lest compensation received.

Where sexual organs like religion
Are but tools of manipulation.

Where physical strength is revered
And inner beauty is shunned.

Where heroism is attributed to the wealthy
And power struggles bring new world wars.

Seems intelligence was traded for technology.

Look!

There goes another walking barrel of waste
Contaminating the gene pool.

At this rate of descent,

We'll be in caves by Christmas.

Tobacco Ritual

I really dig the quiet mornings

…after the coffee pot is silenced,
Steam choked out of its manufactured throat
Like a power plant on strike

…after the snap of my thumb
Across the red Bic lighter,
Charring the paper to sizzle the tobacco

…after the tiny blue pilot in my furnace
Ignites into a sudden row of blue flames
Like a runway to Hell

Tranquility

At my kitchen table

I sit
I stare
I sip
I smoke
I know

This is the closest to peace
I'll ever be in a city

With the invisible breath of God

Whirling about my head

Lazy Dreams

When you're jobless
You don't make requests or demands

Deemed undesirable
Without the working man's calloused hands

Maybe you've done good deeds
Maybe you've only dreamt it

Labeled ignorant of industry
With lazy unattainable dreams

They push you out the door
A return to the ice cold streets

As they crackle and crunch
With every step, beneath your feet

On your journey back to nowhere
You think of champagne glasses colliding

You think of romance beside a fire

You think of the Sun
It shares the warmth of a lover's kiss

You think of the Sun
So promising and permanent

You think of the Sun

You think of the Sun

I Never Forget the Faces

I never forget the faces

The appellations may dissolve

Like my faculties in time

…but the faces

Of fragile youth

Of aged splendor

Even the unparalleled mug of an outcast (You're not alone)

Never diminish entirely

Nor do memorable smiles

Lose luster like dying stars

But shine on eternally

 In a universal yet negligent mind

So many cultures, countries, and complexities

In the birthright titles

One cannot be frowned upon

Should names be consigned to oblivion

For of acquaintances, friends, and lovers alike

I never forget the faces

The Art of Bullying

Life like poetry
Can't exist without sorrow

No one is exempt

Even gorgeous ladies
And gallant gents
Have been held in disdain
By an authority or an elder

The art of bullying

Perhaps the drive
Behind all free-thinking artists

Through the ages
The charismatic and popular
Were elevated in society
Those who couldn't differentiate
Between a poster and a painting,
A newspaper and a novel,
Classic music and classless pop
Seem to be the frontrunners
In this culture of coercion

Unable to think on their own
They cannot create
But muscular bodies,
Endless discord,
And disease

They cannot create real art

Or anything of beauty

I too felt the mockery
For being different,
For average looks,
Or either of the two

You see, it doesn't require
A long period of torture
It was but one year for me
My 11th in school
Unsportsmanlike uncool
The gym class fool

The art of bullying

Made a masterpiece of me

I burned inside
But my vengeance was freedom

…and a phoenix arose

From the ashes of my obscurity

Zombies are Popular Now

My parents were divorced
By the time I'd reached 3rd grade
And every other weekend
When I saw my father
He'd take my brother and I
To the video store
Thus began my fascination in film
2 hour excursions
In fantasy and perversion
Zombie films in particular
Even then I was wise
To the flaws in mankind
George Romero gave an escape
Showed us the future
Still too ignorant to see
Though zombies are popular now

In "the Night" we began our descent

In "the Dawn" we were awakened to our demise

In "the Day" we'd the sour taste of betrayal

In "the Land" we gazed into the eyes of the
enslaved

Though zombies are popular now
There are hundreds of books, films,
And television shows on the subject
They're about as played out
As men who hangout in gyms
Hollywood vampires

Or corporate boy bands
Thrown together for pre-teens
And simple minded adults alike

George hadn't a clue
Of his celluloid prophecy

But zombies are popular now
And modern films
No longer aid in my escape
And I don't have to watch *The Walking Dead*
I see them everyday
In the streets, in cars, supermarkets
Walking, driving, talking
Zombies
Trodding aimlessly through existence
Lusting only for flesh
And the power it holds

They wouldn't know what to do with a brain

The Book of Job (The Lawnmower Man)

Every now and then
I call into question
God's motives
Though I've gotten no response
Or perhaps
I'm simply wasting words
Spitting at the empty sky

"Why do I suffer?"

I know I have not
Always walked a straight line
But I cannot say
It was crooked either
And on occasion
I've cursed the creator
In regards to my existence
Though I've often been kind
To friends and strangers
They seemed to surround
That goofy sedated slave

I knew there was more to life
Than what I was force-fed
Even in those days
So I found truth in literature
Or perhaps
The truth found me
I studied the ways and beliefs
Of the Native people

Of my homeland or otherwise
Of world philosophy, poetry
And anthropology

Through all of this knowledge
I found that my life
Your life
Everyone's life
Was completely false
A lie
A cover-up
Of a cover-up
And people began
To distance themselves
From my new thoughts
My new philosophy
From me altogether

I am Job
The Lawnmower Man
The slave
The fool
The clown of your contempt

Remember when you laughed
Now my mind has surpassed you

God told me we're all fucked

Now look whose laughing

Urinal Cakes and Tampon Bins

Hell is repetition

I know this now
As I sit here with a cigarette
Drinking coffee in my kitchen
Dwelling upon the succession of sorrow
I've adopted as a life or existence
I'm leaning toward the latter

I suppose I've been around
I've had as many jobs
As years on Earth
I don't question the meaning of life
Only my role in it
Cast out to be cast the outcast
This can't last
From the board to the deep end
And sinking fast

I know this now
As sit here slumped over, burned out
Like that cigarette butt beside me
It's a repeat performance
Hell is repetition, not change
Like urinal cakes and tampon bins
It's the same all over
Piss is yellow, blood is red
And my toilet still flushes clockwise
All I'd hoped for
Was a little magic
To break up the monotony
Of manufactured man

But that's the downfall of a dreamer
Surrounded by sleepwalkers

I know this now
Life's not a God damn Shakespeare novel
Othello died along with romance
I'm unsure of its return
Heaven is change for the better
For the soul to unlearn
That history was written by the winners
Bloodshed to brainwashing
This can't last
Save a tree, destroy the vision
But Hell is repetition
In high definition
Like urinal cakes and tampon bins
It's the same all over

Now if you'll excuse me
I have to go wash the stains of time
From my hands again

The Irony of it All

I saw a man running in the street.
The expression on his face
Was that of a man awake during a prostate
examination,
That of excruciating pain.

He was sweating profusely
And constantly looking down
At his wristwatch
Perhaps to keep time,
Or perhaps he was late for something,
Or maybe he knows time is running out too.

Either way it was a cold morning
And we're of the few.
The early morning hopeless
Hoping to rise with the Gods
Instead of broken thoughts
And nagging questions.

I think to myself
"Here's a man really trying,
Running
Instead of watching it on television."

All this as I drive past him
Puffing madly on a cigarette.

Frank Zito Lives!

I had a rose delivered
To her place of work

She hung the phone up on me

Just like her man does to her

Perhaps with me
She feels in control
Having none in her life otherwise

Like Frank
I take the abuse

For all the good women
Are either taken or dead
The rest just fill the streets
Like seagull shit
And cigarette filters

So I pour another glass of wine
And toast to my empty life

Here's my fucking Valentine

A dull evening

With a sharpened knife

1876

I long for simpler times
Like 1876,
100 years before my birth

One could differentiate
Between ladies and whores
In these early stages
Of wealth-defined worth

Deals were sealed
With handshakes and spit
In lawless townships
Over poker games, staking claims
Fearing the hangman's grit

Now we've overcrowded prisons
And whores can run companies
Inadequate are the pimps
Middle men join the middle class
In the unenjoyment line
And the affluent elite
Are seen as heroes
With laws stacked against you
Discarding loyalty
Lavish, lustful
The sole beneficiary

I've read of simpler times
Like 1876,
100 years before my birth

Before the birth of legal tender

Presidents plastered upon paper
With debts attached to every one
Payable only to the lender

Simpler times

The Gold Rush
The adrenaline rush
The rush of the blood to the penis
The rush of opiates intravenous
As cure for diseases

Now we all have the Dead man's hand

…so don't turn your back to the door

The Thousand Yard Stare

I've got the thousand yard stare
But I was never a field Marine
I've never even served
But a higher power
Still I can gaze
At any given moment
On any given day
And mentally collapse
Into a hallucinatory state
Blurring the outlines
Of life's design
A whirlwind of thoughts
Completely out of focus
In an attempt to grasp
Even a fragment
The worst come first
As I dwell in my private Hell
And a heart that dies of thirst
Sometimes a notion of contentment
Slips into the reel unedited
Engulfed by a war syndrome
The war in my mind

I've got the thousand yard stare
I've been in the shit too long
Though I was never a field Marine
I've never even served

But in 37 years
It's been one Hell of a battle
I've bayoneted hearts
And sewn holes upon my own

Burned bridges to ash
Foiled assassinations of character
And slapped the face of corruption

So where's my medal?

Ghost Town Grandeur

I must admit
It gives me great pleasure
To see ghost towns,
Abandon buildings
Overrun with vegetation,
Covered in kudzu
As opposed to being overgrown
With foolish people,
Useless trinkets,
And plastic playthings.

Ah….and how wretched
Most of them are.
Always the perverted, who preach,
Poisonous penises,
Snakes of Eden
And pseudo-scientific know-it-all's
Sucking at life
From the shadows
Of mommy's breast.

Why, if people were rewarded
For their foolishness,
The numbskulls would be boasting about,
Ribbons upon their waxed chests, insipid
And strutting with stupidity.

So I smile
To see ghost towns,
Valleys unfold
As I cross summits and descend
Into moss covered rocks

Strewn about endless fields,
Surrounding pristine ponds
And unpaved paths, forged
By animal or Native man
Lest tire tracks and toxicity
Symbolic of the enemy
Of our great mother.

Here the paper chasers have fled
Into the depths of plastic city.

Here no trees have bled

Here I feel no pity.

Prosperity Program

I've tasted no fruits in my labor
Mere trickery to enslavement
New wage and promise
Birthed a new age doubting Thomas
A sour palate
Resembling rotting vegetables
And maggots upon the meat
Lest they join the hunt
With tasteless tongues numb
Utter nonsensical newsfeed
Pre-written, scripted
To pass off as reality
But by this time
A drug-addled brain, fermented
Remnants of an empty stomach
Keeps one going through the motions
Like a blind gerbil
Running a prosperity program
For I know no other

My World, My Rules

Many times in my life
I've run into many vindictive people
Their feeble minds can't sustain
A decent conversation without antagonizing
Or spitefully disagreeing with you
Only to contradict themselves immediately

So I'd decided long ago
To live inside my head
By my own set of rules
Opposite of them all
No teams, no sides, no programs
All passion, no fashion

Petrified driftwood

In a sinking civilization

Soul of a Steel Horseman

There's no greater feeling
No greater high
Ballin' that Dodge at 85

Taking even the sharpest turns
Foot clung to acceleration
One hand upon the wheel

Burning cigarette dangling
From the appendages of the other

Burning the weathered twisting
Mountain road southbound

Every straight-away
Gun the machine
Take it up 10 more
Ride hard, ride fast, ride free
Upon the highway unforgiving
Unconcerned of consequence

For there's no greater feeling
No greater high
To feel the rubber grip asphalt
As it curls beneath
My line of vision

Only to fade away
From the rearview instantaneously
Like distance lovers past
Charred bridges and stones cast
Draggin' that line

Pulling me toward destiny

Toward something

Déjà Vu

I've been swimming with sharks again
With a harpooned heart
Beer-battered
For the bigger fish to fry

It's all strangely familiar

Shit-canned from another job
Beguiled by big business

Unemployment cut without warning
Bamboozled by Big Brother

It's all strangely familiar

Consumed by desire for a wedded woman
An easy target, my open heart

Climbing the walls with a madness
Dream delirium, my sanity in question

Strangely familiar

Mutants congest fast food joints

Bastards continue to breed

The vilest delve into political science

The children of tomorrow cannot write
Nor have the capacity to read

Strangely familiar

I've stepped out of the flesh parade again
Deflated the ego
Cut the strings
For the puppet master's amusement

Loyal subjects dance above me
Low down, rock bottom, and blue
Facedown in shit
As the wheel of life spins on
Like 5 empty chambers
In the cylinder of a snub-nose

Only one way left to go

Hollywood, New York D.C
(District of Cocksuckers)

I hear it all the time
People babbling about
Praising actors, newscasters
Or anyone on the big screen
Doesn't matter the level of talent
Or if any at all
But eggshell teeth
Six-pack abs
And chests like wax sculptures

I say it all the time
I've seen better acting off-screen

At places of employment

At bars and pubs

Markets and holiday gatherings

In friends and family

Whores and housewives

Politicians, pigs, and priests

In fact
Most people are acting
Through most of their lives
They need a mask
To face their fear

That the one lying next to them
Could've won an Oscar

As I pour another cup of coffee

I know that somewhere

Someone's fucking their way to the top
Unbeknownst to their spouse

A lawman's abusing his power
Dampening the streets in a small town

The left wing are golfing with the right
Sun shining on their fat wallets

…and the Dalai Lama's watching the Today show
Eating a bowl of cornflakes
In a lavish apartment

Bravo!

Take a Bow, Show's over

The Gods clap with a thunderous roar
Looking down
Applauding the audacity
Of the sickening circus
They've created
Often times it's accompanied
By tears of laughter, of joy
Raining down upon us all
Sustaining that bitterness
We've grown accustomed

Can one blame them?
Idiotic assholes are elevated
Into positions of power
The kind you can't wipe clean
And flush away the corruption

It's a real freak show down here
A cultureless whorehouse erected
By phony forefathers, false flags
And slave trade
Packaged as progression
For us peasants
And the wealthy have the gall
To play God with the lives
They've already bought and sold
To a point where I tire
Of the turning wheel
The cycles are stale
Or perhaps I am old

As the Gods clap with a thunderous roar

Looking down
Laughing at the faux pas farm
Stomping their feet upon Heaven's floor
It's unfortunate few are listening
So I pray they cast down lightning

To resuscitate the hearts of us all

Beneath the Floorboards

…and here I lie
Unsatisfied

Claim no side
Yet outlast them all
Unnoticed

Above tarnished brass fittings,
Copper pipes and cobwebs

Beneath the tile,
Rotting planks and rusted nails

Discolored by the dross
Of your couch stains and quarrels

I hear it all
Unresponsive

Like a man who'd died in slumber
An invalid at a pageant

Yet through the shame
I remain
My listless expression
Unchanged

Convictions
Unswayed

As you act out your drama
Of commonplace dreams and inborn fear

Just as the simpletons prior
They stomp out the oddities

Splintered…
Nailed…
Impaled…
Beneath the floorboards

…and here I lie
Unsatisfied

The Drink

"A woman can drive you insane"
Said my father

Headfirst into the psych ward
All the while
Their legs are wrapped around another

…and if they're not
The mere thought of it consumes you

A man on the brink
Thus our thirst
For "the drink"

She's probably lying
Beside another blind sap right now
Spewing the same
Post-sex promises
   Of her innocence and allegiance
      Of hopes and the sweetest dreams
         Of future rendezvous

…and I took the bait
Hook, line, and sinker
We hooked up
I fell for her lines
And now I sink

Perfect time
For "the drink"

Countless men have been destroyed

Or destroyed themselves
Seems love's the missing link

So I continue on
For the moment I stop to think

I long to taste

"The drink"

A Heart's Calling

If you have a moment of silence
Listen closely
You can hear your heart calling

Often times it can push
The clouds of trapped feelings

Or it can fill you
With that weightless joy

To be the Sun
Of another heart's setting
The center of a soul galaxy

Every now and then
If you've a moment of calm
You can feel the passion

Like a passing comet
Blinding to the eye
Soothing to the senses
Should you catch it
Before it's exit

You'll find love is like driving
Through the desert without headlights
You never know what lies ahead

…and everything else falls to shadow
But the stars of Heaven's highway

…and the one that shimmers

In the reflection of the crystalline tears

As they drop and dissolve
From your loving eyes

Thoughts will manifest with emotions

…and you'll smile each day you arise

Good Luck

I make friends easily
I always have

Because I'm real

Whether those I meet wear a mask
I cannot say

But I have nothing to hide
Nor fear

Though I dispute the beliefs
Of the silent flock, status quo
I adapt to change like a chameleon

Born against
The grain and injustice
I question everything

Because I'm real

Amidst the plastic phonies
Of progression

To live this way in unreality
Obstacles can be overwhelming

You may awaken one day alone
Or not wake up at all

For if not silenced by fear
They'll go to great lengths

To make you disappear

Ask a descendant of JFK

…if you can find one

3 Day Old Pizza

3 day old pizza
and it's rent week

…and the wind rattles
The lead painted windows

The lifeless march to their masters
The living smile on in their caskets

Unfazed, Unmotivated
People ask why I'm always laughing
But if they knew what I know
They wouldn't take it all so seriously

I long for companionship
Just like anyone else
and modern women still drive me mad
but when I live with them
They want me to change
Then I miss living alone
With my cat

My heaping ashtray

My bottle

The soothing sounds of Latin jazz
Anytime I choose

My bed

My 3 day old pizza

Though I still love to cook

But it's rent week
So I'll parade with the lifeless for a bit

As the living smile on in their caskets

The Comedy Show

I'd been back in Buffalo roughly 2 years
When my friend Greg came up from Atlanta
On a comedy tour

We'd graduated in the same class
And half of the bastards were there
The place was packed
Huddled into their little cliques

Just like school

All but 2 women ignored me

Just like school

All but 2 men acknowledged my presence

Just like school

They see me as a ghost
A lowdown loser
They've a small town mentality

Just like school

Greg stole the show that night
And I sat at the bar alone
Back to them all

Not unlike the old days
I'm glad they avoid me
Not much has changed

Only now
They have houses and spouses

Only now
I'm not afraid to send them all to Hell

The Reaper's Dance

As the faucet drips
And the slumlord won't return my calls
Not unlike the last time
The biblical deluge from the frozen pipes
Burst in the basement
I think of bodies floating
In rivers of filth

As the cat sits upon the table
Trying to put an end
To the dance of the candle's flame
I admire his valor
To square off with the reaper daily
Like blackened spoons and glass stems
Wasting days, wasting away

But that's not my scene
And I don't have 9 lives
But I do dance with death on occasion
Like blackout drunk driving and falling in love

Though I never think to ask him
Which has ruined more lives?

Which will ruin mine?

City Side Up

The city can soften a man
Like mold on vegetables
Out of the sheer convenience
Of everything, handed down
Delivered and sold
Minds into mush
Bodies not much better off
Everything's on TV
Remote controls, delivery fees
Ill at ease
But the false bravado
Of the phony tough
We're taught to portray
Will land you a rung
On a corporate ladder
Or a ring on a spouse
To grow to despise
Who you really are
A soft-boiled hollow man
With a paper heart
Going through the motions
Clinging to the convenience
Softened from the city
Helpless without it

Letter from the City

6:42 AM

I hear the garbage truck
Coming down the street

But it's 2 days past
The designated day
For pick-up

Seems my neighbor downstairs
Didn't know either

They must have informed us
In the letter I received
From the city

The one I threw away unopened
As I do with all mail

From attorneys,

Cities,

States,

Debt collectors,

Slumlords

Anything that'll drag me down
In an attempt
To contain my fire

Today is the Tomorrow of Yesterday's When

As credulous children we had not a worry
Unconcerned of consequence, befuddled
As dividing lines are blurry

Today is the tomorrow of yesterday's when

Our conduct scrutinized under watchful eyes
Complacent with false education, blind
To the carpetbagger's common guise

Today is the tomorrow of yesterday's when

To come of age means not of form
Despite visible atrophies, assured
Where deprivation is the norm

Today is the tomorrow of yesterday's when

Earth to rebirth

Souls among men

Play it again!

She played me like a used harmonica
All saliva and cover songs in blue

Echoing the same words
Like scratches on vinyl
We can't rewind, only repeat
As life spins on

Once again I was fooled
Into a rhythm
The sweet sounds of passion
Breath on skin
Beating hearts
The drums of desire

When I lie awake at night
I know time heals nothing
I lift the needle from the record
And still hear her song

Play it again

Your cover songs in blue
You're dead to me now and I pray

That I

…am dead

…to you

Into the Darkness

Into the darkness
Drowning in it
Enveloped by it

A denizen of dark bars
The sour stench
And stale conversation

Soul painted black
Words expressed
And the sound of revolution

Drawn to the darkness
And the demons therein
A disgrace of God

A citizen of space and time
Outlaw unto oblivion
Delving in debauchery

I return to darkness
For upon reaching the light

I found that it burned

Shortcut

I feel dizzy and overwhelmed
Watching people running about
Mindlessly chasing this or that

…and for what?

The rat race

The grey race

The consolidation
Of the human race
The Hollywood face erase

The race to be in space
Leaving the poor below
To scavenge, as we've done
Since we left the starting gate

I've a bum leg
A bum heart
And a bum's life

Seems father time is catching up
And I don't give a damn

I found the shortcut to oblivion

Fire Starter

I fueled the fire and fanned the flames
Extinguished by the face of her fear

I scribbled upon the walls of empty voids
Segues between the scenes of sadness

I stared into the windows of a dream
To awaken in a state of disorientation

I caressed the soft flesh of perfection
Pathway to the halls of euphoria

I filled intrigue with casks of passion
Forbidden nectar of the Heavens

I held in my hands a damaged heart
To be stripped by the grip of indifference

I fueled the fire and fanned the flames
To crawl back into the void

Alone

In pain

Is There Something Wrong With Me?

I don't watch TV, unless on DVD
I can't stand commercials.
My reality's not like the one they display.
I see award shows as merely
Hedonistic talent contests for ugly rich children,
Servants of a secret sect.

Is there something wrong with me?

Sometimes I just sit
And stare at the wall
And think about everything
And nothing.
If my mind were on canvas
I'd be painted Pollock.
An animal abstract expressionless,
Few will over-stand.

Is there something wrong with me?

I call marijuana " the plant of the Gods"
I'm confused by prohibition
I frequent bars and consume whisky.
I solicit strange women,
Though I go home alone
For fear of stalkers
And commitments.
I've dealt with both.

Is there something wrong with me?

I don't play games.
I haven't enjoyed them
Since arcade eradication.
I hate computer generated imagery.
I don't buy into trends,
Nor do I partake in sports.
Rarely will you see me wear shorts
And tight jeans put pressure upon the penis.
Snake suffocation, denim demise.

Is there something wrong with me?

I don't vote,
Nor do I think yours counts.
I find people that stand in line
To cast ballots for unworthy oligarchs
Who care not for your well-being
To be fools.
I claim no political party,
Nor religious denomination.
I tell people that I don't see color in others,
Yet I find women with darker skin than my own
Are sometimes more attractive.

Is there something wrong with me?

Perhaps.

…but at least I'm not you.

2

BLUE COLLAR HOURS

37 Years of Nothing

The first hour has passed

Not much longer I return
To the slave ship

The new guy walking the plank
Point of a scimitar in my spine
Wielded by an arrogant kid
10 years younger

Same old story
Though it's getting harder
To mask the self-inflicted sorrow
As I reach these last chapters

I've no need to turn the page

In 37 years of nothing

Time for emancipation

For my soul to disengage

Breaking Friends

So many times I've tried
To befriend my coworkers
Only to be betrayed
Or stabbed in the back
Often times forewarned
I ignored the advice
Of many, and in every instance
I was given the boot
Or demoted

I look back at my 2 year stint
On the 10th floor
Of a ritzy hotel as a houseman
There was a tough-looking maintenance guy
With a handlebar mustache
They called Irwin
Who was always walking around
With misery carved into his countenance
A man so God damn mean
He probably pissed fire
I thought that was cool

So one day I'd decided
To try to talk to him
"Hey man, how come you never smile?"
He looked at me
With that stone cold listless stare and said
"I'm here to make money, not friends"
As he turned and walked away

Looking back now
That mean son-of-a-bitch

Spoke the truth

I should've been breaking banks
Instead of making ends meet

Seems I'm only breaking friends
For I've no need to compete

Wiseman in a Work shirt

Years ago I dabbled in realty.
It's not what you think.
I did maintenance on apartments
On a team of 8 strung-out looking losers
With no place to go.

I was 25 years old,
They much older.

I despised plumbing calls,
But I liked the button-up blue work shirts
And driving around all day
In the company truck smoking cigarettes.

On a call in one of Buffalo's seedier slums
A co-worker they called Callahan
Approached me
Looking suave with his sleeves rolled up
On his button-up blue work shirt
As he paused and lit a smoke.

He was a thin, high-strung,
Chain-smoking drunk
With a pockmark complexion
Who was always in court
For some drama
With some dame,
So when he told me a story
I tended to listen
As I was impressionable

I stopped what I was doing

And turned to face him
As he exhaled and said,

"Jeff, bang every girl you can!
Because when you're my age,
You're scraping the bottom of the barrel."

Now here I am damn near 40
And I've wasted so much time
Looking for love in mixed-up tricks
Instead of accepting what they were.

I should've listened to old Callahan.

It's dark down here at the bottom of the barrel.

For Losers

Nonchalantly pushing
My 50 gallon garbage can on wheels
Room to room
At the University,
Mind off somewhere
Someplace better
I quietly slip into an administrator's office.
There's a puny little clean-cut man
At the desk reading
The Buffalo news.
I can see him in my peripheral
Setting the newspaper down
Upon his desk when he spoke
"What are doing here?"
I turned and looked at him blankly.
"Um, getting your garbage"

"No, I mean why do you do this job?"

"Um, because I need the money"

"No, I mean you seem like an intelligent guy.
Why are you working here?"

Before I could open my mouth he continued…
"Louis out there…" pointing to my 52 year old
co-worker
Slowly wandering past the doorway.
"He's a loser; this is a job for someone like him"

"Louis a good man!" I replied.

"Yeah he's great, but you have to have something
to fall back on."

I cracked a smile having heard that statement
From my father many years ago.
My response was the same.
"What if I don't want to fall back,
But move forward."

The puny man wasn't amused.
"You ever thought about the military?"

"No, I don't think too much at all."

"Me, I work here, but I'm also a sheriff's deputy
In the town of Arcade."

"Very nice" I said now agitated.

As tied the new liner snug to the can,
I turned and strolled back out
Into the bustle
Of polished suburban students
And tired looking teachers.
Those that he saw as "moving forward".
They didn't seem much different to me,
Only they've never had to live
On Little Debbie
Or buy socks at the dollar store
Or lived in a ghetto.

So I wandered back
To the janitor's closet
For a coffee break with Louis.
As we sat there each day
He spoke excitedly

About the greats of jazz
Arms flailing, cigarette in hand,
Of crazy coked out nights of his youth
With vivid depictions
Of whores past,
Of really living life.

Those "moving forward" would never know
Regardless of degrees and diplomas.

Louis King was my professor
And that closet, my classroom.

Don't Believe Everything That You Think

The ad in the classified section read:

HAVE FUN, GET PAID!

Beneath it was a brief job description
Something about playing with toys
For 40 hours a week
This sounded promising
To a 27 year old stoner
So I dialed the number
And set up a work interview
For the following day

When I'd arrived
A strange frumpy man
With an ugly green button-up shirt
Was waiting for me
At the front door
He greeted me, grabbed my resume
And told me to wait where I stood
Beside his beat-up car

It was a small building
So I thought that perhaps this was the office
And this weirdo was going to drive me
To some vast warehouse
Filled with toys
And unhappy married women
Where we'd sit around all day
And gossip around a table

With toys scattered upon it

Then he returned with a box
Opened his trunk, threw it in
And we were off
As he turned to me
"Now I'll do all the talking
And you'll get the hang of it"
"Sounds good" I replied
Now in full realization
That there was no warehouse
So I asked him
What exactly we did
When suddenly he stopped the car
In front of what appeared to be
A collection agency
Got out, grabbed his box
From the trunk
As I followed him
To the door and inside

3 women sat
Behind a U-shaped reception desk
They smiled as they obviously knew him
As he began his pitch
I'd noticed his voice had a high pitch
A phony tone
I stood there blushing
Looking down at the floor
Raging inside at this embarrassing scene
As inside the box
Were Disney DVD's

A fucking door to door salesman job!

I began to sweat

I needed an escape
But I wanted that free lunch
So I toughed it out
For 4 more agonizing hours
Until he finally stopped
At a fast food joint

I ate and drank
With the gluttony of a Roman King
I felt great
Riding back to the office
With a bloated stomach
And no longer having to hear
His phony sales pitch

He was babbling on
About his wife and the job
As I eased the seat back
Lit a cigarette, cracked the window
And closed my eyes ignoring him

When we'd returned
He parked his car and looked at me
"I really like you, let's go inside
And fill out the rest of your paperwork"

I nodded and stepped out of the car
"I have to get my chapstick
Out of my truck, be right in"

"Okay, see you inside"

I moved quickly to my truck
I must've been parked directly in front
Of the bosses' office
As I saw the strange man walk in

And shake the other man's hand
With a devilish grin
It was some sort of pact
They thought they had me

But I got my free lunch

…and I was driving back home to relax

A Dog without a Day

It was a bitter cold January evening
The kind where you can't differentiate
Between the cigarette smoke
Or the breath you've exhaled

I opened the door
For the lady I'd arrived with
And stepped into the funeral home
It wasn't long after I removed my coat
When I saw them
I could smell the scoundrels
Lingering in their phony air
And bullshit blessings

Awful memories whirled in my head
For 8 months underground I plotted
Like a crazed vigilante
A bitter cold justice
Served in secret

The time had arrived

As not to cause a scene
I stepped to the back
Of the long morbid room
When the heavier of the two
The one who couldn't face me
For my termination 8 months prior
Finally turned
And glanced in my direction
Immediately when he caught sight
Of me, I returned a look

Of pure death
His face became beet red
As he quickly turned away
In his cowardice

My pulse sped up
Like tribal drums
In a ritual sacrifice
This was my day

But as I stood by the door
Waiting to strike
Like a panther in the night
All of the hostile thoughts
Of retaliation and revenge
From the many nights
I'd lie awake feeling hopeless
All seemed to disappear
For when I heard the voice
Of the fat man's puny partner
Directly behind me

"How ya doin?"

My stomach was in knots

My blood burned
Like a vagrant fire
With nothing to live for
Nothing to lose

And my thin angry face
Gave them a look
That would've turned Medusa into stone

Instantly the puny man lowered his head

Scurrying to the door, defeated
Like a lost dog
His larger red-faced companion hurried behind
As not to meet my eyes
But just as he reached the exit
I spoke up

"See you in Hell!"

...and out they went
Into the bitter cold January night

I may not have had my day
But they'll never forget this whistleblower

Till the day they return

To the funeral home for good

Death of a Young Know-it-all

Bathing a canine in a human tub
Scrubs drenched from his movements,
A cocky young tech
Always full of televised wisdom and
misinformation
Who hadn't read a book in his entire life
Crept up and stood beside me.
"How come you don't date man?"
"I do, I just don't talk about it." I replied half
ignoring him,
Dog thrashing about.
"It's cool if you're gay man." He said
Trying to get a rise out of me.
"If you'd dealt with the kind of women I attract,
You'd wish you were gay." I said.
Finally I turned and stared listlessly into his eyes.
"Whatever you think I am or want me to be, I
am."
A look of confusion came over his face
Like I'd spoken an unfamiliar language
As I turned, wrapped the dog in a towel
To begin my descent downstairs to the kennel
I looked back at the young know-it-all.
"Anybody can get laid kid, not everybody finds
love
And love is all you need in this world."
He laughed.
"All I need is money!"
"Money can't buy happiness." I replied.
"No, but it can buy a jet ski."

Feeling the sand in my hourglass

Wither away like his logic
I turned and walked away.

Shortly thereafter
The kid got fired
And I never saw him again.

Three years later
I'd gotten word of his death.
He danced the mainline with Montega
By way of blackened spoon.

Apparently he didn't know too much about livin'.

I hope we're both dealt a better hand next time
kid.

Living the Dream

Sad days start the same,
Dark coffee on cool dark mornings.
But when living check to check,
Week to week
The threads of life
Can unravel rather quickly
Like a cheap sweater
And when I exited
The gas station apparently
The brake hose tore on my truck.
So my arrival to carpool
Left us both late for slavery
(We creatures of the cutting lathe)
Until another man of misery
Picked us up.
As unhappy hours came to end
I was taken back
To the garage for the prognosis.
Still not repaired
I told the mechanic,
"I'll be at the bar across the street."
"Call me when it's done."
I entered and to my amazement
The restaurant portion was empty
But the barstools were filled
With the exception of one space
Beside an unfortunate looking woman
Tumultuously screaming
At a game show
On the television above the bar
Trying desperately
(and rather obnoxiously)

To use her feeble brain
To solve a word puzzle
"Spaghetti!"
"Spaghetti western!"
"Spaghetti!"
Growing louder each time
Turning toward my left ear
As to get the attention
Of another woman to my right.
"Spaghetti!"
"Spaghetti western!"
I signaled the bartender,
"A pint and a shot please!"
Then the disturbed woman turned
To face me again.
"What's a spaghetti western?"
"Old western films were predominately
Made by Italian directors,
Hence the ignorant term spaghetti." I replied.
Suddenly I heard my name.
I turned slowly toward the door behind me,
There stood the mechanic
Greased up in his monkey suit
Holding a brake hose in his left hand.
"Wrong part." he screamed over the loud drunks.
"Thanks man." was all I could mutter
As I turned back around to face the bar.
"Another shot please."
An hour later I could see
It was raining
But not a downpour,
So I paid the tab and stepped out
Into the dampened evening.
I realized at this point
1 cigarette remained in my pack.
I lit that sucker

Pulled the hood on my head
And started home.
As the rain picked up
The temperature went down.
The cold brings sadness,
Sadness brings flashes of memories,
Memory often brings anger.
I pissed behind a dumpster
At a liquor store
And stumbled back
To my apartment.
Will to live exhausted
I removed the sopping wet clothes
And went to bed.

Malaise can last for days
So at night I sleep to dream.

Killing the American Dream, One Check at a Time

Cheaply made in China
Shipped to Canada
Driven to Buffalo
Unloaded and rolled in
Through the dusty warehouse
On a pallet jack
Stacked ceiling high
By me or some other tired fool
Modern day peddlers
Redistributing Chinese goods
To dead Americans
From Sacramento, California
To Boulder, Colorado
Even Rockford, Ohio
At many times the cost

This is the way it works
Our system
Unchecked and unbalanced
The blueprints drawn long ago

…and you'll still wave your flag

…and cast your vote
Because that's all that you know

This it the way it works
I believe not in borders, nor dividing lines
Nor the politicians who create them
So I care not who signs my check

I don't live to work
I work to live

It's all a coin toss anyhow

You're with the Heads of State
Or at the tail end of the breadline
Either way you flip

This is the way it works

Killing the American dream

As it slowly kills me

The Waiting Room

We spend most of our lives waiting

Waiting for new life
To share the stagnant air

Waiting for love
To be swept away, instead of under the rug
For a storybook romance
That simply doesn't exist
Among stockholders and cold shoulders

Waiting for a break
In a chain-gang existence
For more than what's offered

Waiting for legislation
For laws written in your favor
A release for good behavior

Waiting for a program
For an end to commercials

Waiting for acceptance
Among the cliques
Of failed breeders and bottom feeders

Waiting to clock in
For the check, the price
For your vice to keep your balance

Waiting for a handout
For state lottery numbers

And collection plates

Waiting to be noticed
To be envied for your possessions
For your cardboard estates

Waiting for the sick
As they wait for a cure

Waiting for your turn
To be taken care of by another

Waiting for a callous God
A prophet's unlikely return

Waiting to die alone

To be ashes in an urn

Until that day...

Jeffrey Charles Naish

About the Author

Jeffrey Charles Naish began writing poetry as a
confused teenager in search of love and truth just
outside Buffalo, New York. After he finished school
still lost and alone he decided to pack up his
frustrations and venture south. More trials and
tribulations followed until in another moment of clarity
he reached for a pen once more. To date he's published
hundreds of poems and is believed to have returned to
Buffalo.